ISBN: 9798693359161
First English Edition 2020
Translated from Greek by Fragitsa Halkias
All rights reserved
Edited by: Reader Symeon Campbell

Cover design: Chrysostomos Tromboukis, B.A.
www.chrysostomo.wordpress.com

Publisher: Archangels Publications
Retail orders: www.archangelsbooks.com
Wholesale orders: archangelspublications@gmail.com

"Set a guard, O Lord, over my mouth; Keep watch over the door of my lips" (Ps. 141:3).

Archimandrite
Vassilios Bakoyiannis

LION-TAMER

"Archangels Publications" 2020

Apostle James
(3:1-10)

"My brethren, ...if anyone does not stumble in word, he is a perfect man...,

every kind of beast and bird, of reptile and creature of the sea, is tamed and has been tamed by mankind,

but no man can tame the tongue. It is an unruly evil, full of deadly poison.

With it we bless our God and Father, and with it we curse men, who have been made in the similitude of God.

Out of the same mouth proceed blessing and cursing. My brethren, these things ought not to be so".

Let's pray this book makes us a lion tamer...!

CONTENTS

PART I

1. The water tank and the water

If the water of a water tank is clean, it comes out clean. If it is impure, it comes out impure. Likewise, if our heart is pure, our mouth speaks "pure" gentle words. *"A good man out of the good treasure of his heart brings forth good things"* (Mt. 12:35).

And if our heart is impure our mouth speaks harsh words; *"an evil man out of the evil treasure brings forth evil things"* (Mt. 12:35).

So, to understand what a person is hiding in his heart, let him speak. Through his mouth you enter his heart.

"For out of the abundance [1] of the heart, his mouth speaks" (Lk. 6:45). Practically this means that as we pour water in a water tank and as it fills up, it overflows. That which overflows in our hearts comes out of our mouths. In other words, when we speak, we don't "pour out" all (the evil) content of our heart, either out of fear, shame, or both.[2]

However, when we get angry, we lose control, and out of our mouth come forth all the hidden evil. We may scream, curse, and anathematize our children! And after we have calmed down, we would say, *"what happened to me? What did I just say to my children?"*. That is because she was out of control, out of her right mind!

---

[1] The Greek word is "περίσσευμα" which means excess, surplus, abundance.

[2] St. John Chrysostom. Homily 42 on the Gospel by Matthew P.G. 57: 452

Therefore, whatever a man says when he is angry, let's not take it seriously. Consider a priest who rejects Jesus when he is angry; he is not deposed from the office! He is beside himself! [3]

Lastly, a good man out of the surplus of his heart, he speaks by saying good words. If he gets angry, he does not utter shameful words, for such things are alien to his pure heart. He simply will raise his voice, saying a few more words and nothing else.

Can you imagine St. Paisios the Hagiorite uttering blasphemous words when angry?

---

[3] St. Symeon Archbishop of Thessaloniki All his works. Part IV. Question 38.

A parrot may have a mind, but it has no thoughts and no reason. It just imitates, without knowing what it imitates. Thinking is a privilege that only human beings have.

But how our mind formulates a specific sentence?! How does it choose the suitable words?

The same question applies to those who listen to us: How do they understand what we say?! It is a mystery!

2. "No man can tame the tongue"
(Ja. 3:8)

St. Nicodemus the Hagiorite interprets:

Apostle James does not imply that it is impossible to defeat the tongue, but he just wants to emphasize how difficult it is for one to defeat the tongue. "*It is difficult for someone to stop the water flowing into the brook with their hand. It is even much more difficult to tame the tongue.*"[4]

Here some examples from the Fathers of the desert:

Abbas Sisoes: "*For thirty years, I have begged God only for my tongue. Every day I sin in word!*"[5]

Abbas Agathon for three years had a pebble in his mouth, so as not to talk[6]. Imagine how many times he was "bitten" by the beast, to get to the point to put pebbles in his mouth. Not, of course, that he judged, slandered, or insulted anyone, no. Simply, if he had spoken more than he should have, or if he should have kept silent but did not.

Abbas Pambo was illiterate. He did not understand the psalms and attended "private courses." In the first lesson, the teacher analyzed the psalm, "*I will guard my ways, lest I sin with my tongue*" (Ps. 39:1). While Abbas Pambo was listening to the teacher, he thought: "*If I tame my tongue, then I won't need anything else to be saved.*"

Six months passed, and he never went back again to the teacher. Sometime later, the teacher met him and asked:

---

[4] St. John of the Ladder. Step 11 on talkativeness and silence, 10
[5] Gerontikon. Abbas Sisoes, 3
[6] Gerontikon. Abbas Agathon, 15

"Where were you? Why haven't you come again?" And he replied: *"I had to apply what I was taught and to then return. But up to now I didn't manage it!"*

Fifty years had passed since then. They asked Abbas Pambo: *"How did you apply what you learned?"* He answered: *"I've been fighting forty-nine years! And (after 49 years) I managed it! Now I can say, as many times as I spoke, I didn't change my mind."* [7]

"If anyone does not stumble in word, he is a perfect man" (Ja. 3:2).

---

[7] St. Nicodemus the Hagiorite. Explanation on the Psalms. *"Orthodox Kypseli."* Vol. 1st. Thessalonica 1979, p. 556

3. "For every idle word"

"*For every idle word men may speak, they will give account of it in the Day of Judgment*" (Mt. 12:36).
"*For by your words you will be justified and by your words you will be condemned*" (Mt. 12:37).

Let's say that the Government has attached to us a mechanism (like a camera) that records whatever is coming out of our mouths. And we know that if we say a word that is not liked by the Government, that we will pay a fine, for example, one thousand dollars.

What are we going to do? Will we not pay attention to our words? Will we not be vigilant all around the clock? Of course, we will! You see, when there is a reason to bridle the "beast," we can do it if we want...

The Government may not have set up such a mechanism, but God has set it up. He "records" every word that comes out of our mouths. And for every idle and harmful word we speak, we will give account of it in the Day of Judgment (Mt. 12:36). We'll pay a fine, far more expensive than a thousand dollars!

In other words, if we are afraid of the dreadful judgment seat of Christ, "*we set a guard over our mouth; and a watch over the door of our lips*" (Ps. 141:3). Which means, "*whoever doesn't control his words, shows that he does not believe in the*

Lord who says[8]*, "for every idle word men may speak, they will give account of it in the day of judgment"* (Mt. 12:36).[9]

Do we put the bridle to the "beast," or do we leave it free? If we leave it free, it will devour us. It may lead us to Hell...! *"Do not be deceived... nor revilers, will inherit the kingdom of God"* (1 Cor. 6:9-11).

"To slip on the ground is better than the slip of the tongue; thus, the downfall of evil will come speedily" [10] It is better to fall and to get hurt, break your teeth, injure your lips or bleed from your mouth than to say idle words. With a slip on the pavement, your body will get hurt, but with a slip of the tongue, you will damage your soul...!

---

[8] St. Basil the Great. Epistle 51. P.G. 32: 389
[9] St. Basil the Great. Epistle 51. P.G. 32: 389
[10] The Wisdom of Jesus the son of Sirach 20:18

4. After our sin

"*Have mercy upon me, O God... Wash me thoroughly from my iniquity, And cleanse me from my sin. For I acknowledge my transgressions. And my sin is always before me*" (Ps. 51:1-3).

Dear brother, when you are angry, and you're beside yourself, the beast may bite you and injure you. Now the question is, what do you do after the beast has wounded you.

The first thing to do is heal the wound; to show repentance for the sin you committed. Don't stay in the fall but get up. Let your fall be your resurrection. This is what the genuine servant of the Lord does. Here are some examples.

Once, a Monk of the Mount Athos "challenged" the Saint Elder Joseph the Hesychast to discuss a "hot topic" of zealotism (it was a plague on Mount Athos). The Saint Elder answered him: "*Please, let's not discuss this subject. We will say hard words, and we will be sorry.*" The Monk insisted. The Saint began to discuss this hot topic. He was annoyed and uttered hard words against the Monks who followed the zealotism.[11]

Of course, the Elder, after this fall, did not get a rest! Only God knows how many prayers, fasting, vigils, and prostrations he did for this!

Another Saint from Mount Athos, Efraim Katounakiotis, once got angry towards a young Monk from his brotherhood.

---

[11] The Elder Efraim Katounakiotis. Published by Holy Hesychastetion "*St. Efraim.*" Katounakia of Holy Mountain. Pg. 108-109,175.

And he cursed (!) the Monk! *"May you have a bad out-come/life"* (τόν κακό σου τόν καιρό). Immediately, the old Elder fell at the feet of the young monk and apologized to him! *"My child, forgive me! I said a bad word!"* [12]

Imagine an old, white-haired Elder, falling on his feet and begging for forgiveness from his young disciple! And that was just the first step. Who knows what else he did in secret in his cell!

We can, at any time, fall and commit a sin in word. When this happens, we need to replace our fall with a corresponding spiritual struggle; to kneel down in front of the Crucified Lord and beg for His mercy and His forgiveness.

Really, what is the difficulty in doing this?

Do we need to dig or pay taxes or have surgery to do this?

Since it's so easy and so beneficial to our souls, why don't we do it?

---

[12] Ibid. Pg. 108-109.

PART II

1. Our mouth and our passions

"*Those things which proceed out of the mouth come from the heart, and they defile a man*" (Mt. 15:18).

St. John Chrysostom: "*If we throw wild animals into a pit, cover it up so that no air gets in, the animals will die. If, on the other hand, we leave an opening in the pit, the animals will become enraged. This is exactly what happens with our desires. If we express them through the words, they become 'enraged,' and they will overthrow us to the cliff of debauchery. So, if we have evil thoughts, let's close our mouth, and they will quickly die*".[13]
The passions we have inside us feel like we are in prison. They want their freedom; to get out. They're pushing. The easiest way to be released is through our words. They breathe, and they become alive and stronger. That is, every time we open our mouths and say an idle word, we feed our passions. So, if we want to tame our passions, we must first tame our tongue.

They were certain Monks who would say anything that came into their minds. "*Sure! Those Monks are good, but their courtyard does not have a door, and anyone can enter and untie his donkey, which is indispensable for his livelihood,*"[14] an Elder said to St. Anthony the Great. "*Death and life are in the power of the tongue*" (Pr. 18:21).

---

[13] St. John Chrysostom. About the ambiguity of the Old Testament. P.G. 56: 187
[14] Gerontikon. Abbas Antonios, 17

21

"How can we protect our hearts when its main entrance, our tongue, is always open?" asked Sisoes the Great.[15]

The above means: A Christian can struggle with prayers, vigils, great fasting, attending Church, receiving Holy Communion frequently, and confessing his sins, but if he is not careful with what he says and what he hears, his struggle is in vain. He feeds on his own passions, which he struggles to overcome.

"If anyone among you thinks he is religious and does not bridle his tongue but deceives his own heart, this one's religion is useless" (Ja. 1:26).

---

[15] Evergetinos. Vol. IV. Case 24. Chapter I, 6

Once ten frogs set out to overcome an obstacle, they wanted to climb to the top of a big pole. All the sportsmen gathered to observe the spectacle.

They were talking with one another. They said that it was impossible for the frogs to climb the pole and that as soon as they would attempt to climb it, they would be forced to give up the effort.

Amongst all the frogs that attempted to climb the pole, only one managed to climb to the top.

And that frog was deaf...!

2. Our ears and our passions

The Japanese doctor, Dr. Masaru Emoto, after many experiments, had proven that water "understands" what we say! For example, when it hears insulting and offending words against it, it is disturbed! Whereas when it hears words of love, it becomes peaceful![16] And our body consists of 70% water. Accordingly, words affect our bodies. This applies even more for our souls.

St. John Chrysostom: *"What air is to a sailing ship (which is the driving force of a ship), words are to the soul. With words, you can go where you want. You shape your life as you want it! Many good people were led to sinful actions, listening to blasphemous words".*[17]

Think about how much our soul is damaged when we hear shameful words, blasphemy, and slander all of the time!

"Let's not have the illusion that we are not influenced by hearing such words! We are not superior to Eve, who was deceived by the cunning conversation with the snake!"[18]

Improper words shouldn't even be mentioned as a joke; these descend into our subconscious self. Our subconscious self is unable to distinguish between serious and light-hearted and takes matters seriously. This "silently" causes damage to our soul.

---

[16] More about this in his book: *"The Secret Message of Water"* translated by Neli Kouskoleka, Esoptron, 2001

[17] St. John Chrysostom. Homily 2, on Second Epistle to the Thessal. P.G. 62: 478

[18] Abbas Isaac the Syrian. Evergetinos.Vol. 1. Case 22. Chapt. 7th.

It would be better to imitate King David when we are in "bad" company: *"I, like a deaf man, do not hear; And I am like a mute who does not open his mouth. Thus I am like a man who does not hear. And in whose mouth is no response"* (Ps. 38:13-14).

If bad words have such a big impact on our souls, imagine the impact of bad images! *"A picture speaks a thousand words!"*

Once, the following experiment took place. They embedded in a video offensive and disturbing images that flashed so quickly that people didn't have time to realize what they were seeing. Nonetheless, the people seeing this "inconceivable" video became subconsciously anxious! Then they embedded in the video nice and calming images. And the people became subconsciously calm!

Now think of what is going on inside us with the mental pictures conceived in our mind's eye!

"We are what we eat, what we hear, and what we look at."
And then we complain, *"what is life about?"*

3. *"An open tomb"*

*"**L**et no corrupt word proceed out of your mouth, but what is good for necessary edification, that it may impart grace to the hearers"* (Eph. 4:29)

The Scripture calls the throat *"an open tomb"* (Ps. 5:9). Because the opened tomb (not the closed) smells bad. So, it is with an uncontrolled mouth. It smells! *"Don't you see how the pigs chew and eat dirty things? So, do those who have an uncontrolled mouth. Is there anything dirtier than words coming out of our mouths? Whoever has such a mouth is dirtier than a dog that has just vomited!"* [19]

And the stench of the opened tomb is not only felt by the one who opened the tomb, but also by those around him. So, it is with another "opened tomb," the mouth, by saying blasphemous words. They do not only defile those who say these words, but they also defile those who hear these words! [20] *"Those things which proceed out of the mouth come from the heart, and they defile a man"* (Mt. 15:18).

A charismatic Elder attended a conversation held by the Monks. When the discussion focused on spiritual and heavenly things, an Angel descended from heaven praising the Monks. And when the discussion focused on earthly and vain things, it

---

[19] St. John Chrysostom, Homily 31 on Acts. P.G. 60: 233
[20] St. John Chrysostom, about the ambiguity of the Old Testament P. G. 56: 187

was like pigs came and wallowed in mud, and spread the stench polluting the Monks![21]

And the Monks didn't insult or speak smut! Even though their company was like a pigsty!

Think about what happens to a group of people *"who insult and speak smut! Demons are coming!"*[22]

The same is true in the homes where people swear, say blasphemous words, and watch various sinful things on television and the internet. The demons are coming. This home has a stench! (It needs Holy Water).

"Fill, my dear, your mouth with aroma and not with stench. Make your mouth a treasure of goods, not a place of demons." [23]

---

[21] Evergetinos. Vol. 2nd. Case 47. Chapter Second, 10

[22] St. John Chrysostom. Homily 32 on the Gospel of John P. G. 59: 187

[23] St. John Chrysostom. About the ambiguity of the Old Testament P. G. 56: 187

4. Words damage body

"*My son, do not forget my law, But let your heart keep my commands; For length of days and long life And peace they will add to you*" (Pr.3:1-2).

The Galatians complained amongst themselves, and Paul characterized this "grumbling" as bites of one to another...! "*But if you bite and devour one another, beware lest you be consumed by one another!*" (Gal. 5:15). What do we say when someone nags us? We say: "*He has eaten me alive.*"

A psychiatrist once said that when we become angry, our psychic world disperses toxins; the tongue "*is full of deadly poison,*" James says (Ja. 3:8). These toxins are poisonous and dangerous to our health. At that moment, our words are mixed with this poisonous substance, and we "serve" these poisonous words to our fellow human beings. In so doing, we bring poisonous toxins into his psyche, and we poison him! "*You poisoned us*" (μᾶς φαρμάκωσες) our fathers used to say whenever they heard harsh words.

Recall; Our body changes when we hear insulting and offensive language against us. It means: Our body does not only become sick from microbes or pollution, cold or bad nutritional habits but also from listening to blasphemous words! (Who knows, maybe in the future medical science will discover that, e.g., the sin of reproach causes this disease! Who knows!)

So, do you want to stay healthy? Watch your ears and your mouth, especially.

Experiments have proven this. It has also been shown by the experience of our Holy Fathers. For example, St. Symeon, the

New Theologian, said: *"The words of the saints, as well as prayer, make the body healthier and stronger."*[24]

The same was said by the contemporary Saint Porphyrios Kavsokalivitis: *"I pay great attention to the reading of the Bible and attending Church Services. You are being healed without comprehending it."*

"Who is the man who desires life, and loves many days, that he may see good? Keep your tongue from evil, and your lips from speaking deceit" (Ps. 34:12-13).

---

[24] All his works. Part I. Logos 76. Published by "Regopoulos". Thessalonica 1969, p. 415

PART III

1. Neither your eyes nor your ears

Don't trust your eyes nor your ears. They deceive you! *"From what you hear, don't believe in it,"* say the people. Our ears hear what we have in our minds. For instance, if you have the number "two" in your mind, and you hear the word "too," your mind believes it heard the word "two!" Therefore, don't believe anything bad you hear about your brother, and especially don't spread it as it may be "fake news." *"You shall not circulate a false report"* (Ex. 23:1), says God.

He (God) told Abraham: *"I will go down now and see whether they have done altogether according to the outcry [25] against it that has come to Me; and if not, I will know"* (Gen. 18:21). He also visited Sodom and Gomorrah to determine if everything that He had heard was true about these cities. He wanted with this (as St. John Chrysostom states) to persuade us that *"we should not condemn sinners without having proof, but to examine everything with great care."* [26]

The same is valid with our eyes. They see what we have in our mind, and not what is really going on!

---

[25] Our sins become an outcry to God because His commandments are violated. God said to Cain *"The voice of your brother's blood cries out to Me from the ground"* (Gen. 4:10). Think of how many cries the Lord hears from the sins of all humankind!

[26] St. John Chrysostom. Homily 42 on Genesis P.G. 54: 389

It is said that a Monk had the feeling that two Monks from his Monastery were homosexuals. While it was still dark outside, this Monk came out from the Monastery to do his assignment.

He thought that he saw, in the field near the Monastery, these two Monks one on top of the other! *"Oh..."* he said, *"I caught them in the act!"* He ran to the Monastery and informed the Elder. They hurried to catch them *"by the door."* As they approached, they saw two bundles of wheat, one on top of the other, covered with a black blanket...! *"From what you see, believe half of it,"* as is common saying amongst the people.

Whenever Alexander the Great was listening to accusations against someone, he covered one of his ears with his hand. They asked him. *"Why are you doing this?"* and he answered: *Because with the other ear, I want to hear the accused; things might not be as I hear them now!"*

And yet we listen to the accusations about others with both ears! We are more attentive to such accusations than to the Holy Gospel...!

2. "Fake news"

*T*eacher! I would like to tell you something that I heard? Someone once said to Socrates.
- *Have you researched it well and would say this is true?*
- *No!*
- *Would I benefit by listening to it?*
- *No!*
- *Do I need to know it well?*
- *No!*
- *Then forget it. Let's say something true and useful instead!*
And Socrates lived before Christ; in darkness. May we who live after Christ, think, in this case, as Socrates thought; nevertheless, we don't ...

Well. Neither our eyes nor our ears must be trusted. But in fact, we trust our eyes and our ears. And whatever negative thing we hear or see about our brother, without checking whether it was accurate, we say it to others![27]And we don't say it exactly just as we heard it or as we saw it, but we cook it and put a lot of sauce on top!

And this is happening only for what we hear negative about our brother in Christ! While when we hear something good, we do not spread it! Our passions are nourished only by such things! It's like a fly that is attracted to dirt, always looking for the bad things in life...!

---

[27] Since *"no man can tame the tongue"* (Ja. 3:8), there are no secrets...! Think: When we are listening to something "interesting", we are under pressure to spread it to the others. And if something is "secret" we are more pressured to say it to others! *"To be a secret, two must know it, but one of them must be dead"* (Folk saying).

Think of the sin we do by spreading what negative things we hear about our brother. We light fires! *"Don't start fires,"* advised our fathers to their children. *"Even so the tongue is a little member and boasts great things. See how great a forest a little fire kindles!"* (Ja. 3:5). God will hold us responsible for the souls that were burned...!

Some (more dangerous) people have psychological problems. They cannot separate reality from the imagination. For example, they can imagine that their neighbor killed their brother, and they refer to this as a real fact! *"This neighbor killed my brother!"*

These people recite the "fact" as if it is a fairy tale, which is why they always fall into contradictions. If you ask them, *"When and how did that occur?"* they will either be embarrassed, or they will say other things now and something else later because they haven't seen anything, in fact.

3. "A sharpened sword"

"*People* inside are like wounds that never heal, no matter how many bandages we use," an Elder said. Good words relieve people, whereas hard words hurt them. "*Your words are sharper than your sword*" (Shakespeare). Can we realize it? "*Deliver me, O Lord, from evil men...they sharpen their tongues like a serpent; the poison of asps is under their lips*" (Ps. 140:1-3).

A young man was helping a grandfather. He went to the forest to cut wood and loaded it onto his donkey. This was done many times. One day the young man said to the grandfather:
- *Tell me, how do you see me?*
- *My child, you have a thousand good qualities. You are loving, handsome, and kind, but you have one bad trait: Your mouth has a stench!*
The young man went to the forest after a few days, helping the grandfather again. As they were about to leave, he said to the grandfather:
- *Cut my hand with your knife.*
- *Oh...! I can't...!*
- *Please do that for me! There is a reason. The young man insisted again and again!*
And the grandfather with the heavy heart cut the young man's hand!

After a few days, the grandfather returned into the forest. The young man also went to the forest to help him again. He said to the grandfather:
- *How does my hand look?*
- *Fine! The wound closed!*

- Yes! But another wound still bleeds, which you have opened in my heart! You said that my mouth has stench! Get away from here, for I will kill you.

He forgot all the praises (you are loving, handsome, and kind) that the grandfather had told him, and he got stuck on *"your mouth has a stench!"*

"A sharpened sword" calls the Scripture the tongue of evil people. *"Who sharpen their tongue like a sword and bend their bows to shoot their arrows-bitter words"* (Ps. 64:3).

Such a knife we all have, and we always have it out of the pouch...!

4. A good word

"*The* good man when he hears a bad word, he becomes a bad man. The bad man when he hears a good word, he becomes a good man!*"* [28]

St. Macarius of Egypt was going up to Mount Nitria, along with another fellow Monk, who was walking ahead of the Saint. As they were moving along, an idolater priest ran into the Monk. *"O! Demon! Where are you running to?"* said the Monk. The idolater priest got angry and hit the Monk, leaving him unconscious. The priest continued running down his way, where he ran into St. Macarius.
- *"I wish you all right; I wish you all right...!"* The saint said.
- *"What good did you find in me that you talked like that?"* The idolater asked the Saint.
- *"You work hard,"* said the Saint.
- *"When you greeted me, I felt something in my heart. I understood that you are a man of God. I will not leave you unless I become like you!"* And he knelt and embraced the feet of the Saint.
The idolater priest was baptized as a Christian and then became a tonsured Monk. Because of this, many idolaters were baptized Christians.

Have we thought about what reward St. Macarius had received from God, only by saying a good word which yielded these results?

---

[28] Gerontikon. Abbas Macarius, 39

The same is true for us. Whenever we say a good word, and by that word someone is led to repentance, God will reward it to us by covering *"a multitude of sins"* (Ja. 5:20).

And this reward will be given when only one man is led to repentance. If two men repent, the reward will be greater! If three men repent, the reward will be even greater and so on!

The opposite is also true. Consider what "reward" a Christian will have if, with a shameful word, someone is led to sin, *"it would be better for him if a millstone were hung around his neck, and he were drowned in the depth of the sea"* (Mt. 18:6).

And what reward he will have if two men are led to sin and so on!

It is said that there was an author who wrote many sinful books. He died and went to Hell! After his death, the more his books were read, the more his punishment increased in Hell...!

5. Woman and nagging

- *Dad, are you afraid of crocodiles?* Asked a young boy.
- *No...!*
- *Are you afraid of tigers?*
- *No...!*
- *Lions?*
- *No...!*
- *Is mom the only thing you're afraid of, dad?*

Pay attention: The devil, as soon as he convinced Eva to eat the fruit, didn't go to Adam; he left matters in Eve's hands. (Gen. 3:1-6). He knew that Eve could manage better, and she succeeded...!

The devil killed all of Job's animals, all his shepherds, all his children, and their spouses, except Job's wife...![29] And this was not because he loved her, but as St. John Chrysostom says, to make Job turn against God! [30]

Women tend to be emotional beings by nature. This helps them to be more compassionate. However, they must be vigilant and guard their hearts against talkativeness. St. Gregory, the

---

[29] *"Suddenly a great wind came from across the wilderness and struck the four corners of the house, and it fell on the young people, and they are dead"* (Job 1:19). *"He took for himself a potsherd with which to scrape himself while he sat in the midst of the ashes. Then his wife said to him, "Do you still hold fast to your integrity? Curse God and die!""* (Job 2: 8-9).

[30] More: Archimandrite Joel Giannakopoulos. The Old Testament according to the Seventy. Vol. 8. Job. "Lydia Publications", 1986. Pg.15-16.

Theologian, wrote to the newly married Olympiada: *"Your husband will be your enemy if you do not harness your tongue, regardless if you possess a thousand gifts."*

King Solomon, by his experience, has said: *"Better to dwell in the wilderness, than with a contentious and angry woman"* (Pr. 21:19). *"It would be better if my wife were to slaughter me with a knife rather than saying such heavy words to me,"* a husband had once confessed to me.

"What a beautiful woman you have!" said a young man to his friend, and he answered, *"I cannot stand her anymore! She has tormented me with her nagging."*

The opposite is also valid. *"What an ugly wife you have!"* said one friend of mine to a husband. *"No! No! My wife is an earth angel!"* His wife was meek and calm. *"A gentle tongue breaks a bone"* (Pr. 25:15).

"He who finds a (good) wife finds a good thing and obtains favor from the Lord" (Pr. 18:22).

6. Body language

It is not enough to say good words to someone, but we must also say them in a good way. *"7% of our spoken words themselves affect our listener. 38% is through the tone of our voice. 55% through our body language."* (Albert Mehrabian)

Research has shown that when we praise someone with a cold heart, it is as though we are blowing pessimism into his soul despite the good words said to him! On the other hand, when we point out someone's defects with a warm heart, we encourage him despite our negative criticism!

All this to say that our body language is more important to convey something to our fellow man than words themselves, no matter how good they are. *"You are hurling golden crowns with diamonds at people, but the way you're throwing them, you are hurting heads, not just sensitive ones, but hard ones, too,"* said St. Paisios, the Hagiorite to a missionary, who said useful words in an improper manner.[31]

Saint Silouanos, the Hagiorite, cites his personal experience. Before he became a monk, he was in his village. Being a young man, he was living a sinful life. The Mother of God appeared to him, saying: *"I don't like your works!"* Those words, though they were "offensive," woke him up! And he never forgets this incident! He wrote: *"Forty years have passed since then, and I can't*

---

[31] Words of St. Paisios. Volume 2nd. Published by *"Holy Monastery Evangelist John the Theologian"*. First edition. 1999. Pg.78

forget that sweet voice! I do not know how to thank the Mother of God." [32]

Another incident was when he had sinned with a young woman from his village one night. His father knew what was going on that night with his son. Early in the morning, the young Symeon (this was his layman name) came home. Then his father asked him: *"Oh, my child! Where were you last night? My soul was in great pain!"* Saint Silouan remembered these words throughout his life! [33]

A wise man is not the one who says wise things, but the one who knows when he must speak and how to speak.

---

[32] The writings of St. Silouanos. Chapt.11 about the Mother of God. Archim. Sofronios. St. Silouanos. Edition 8th. Essex 1999.Pg. 493
[33] Archim. Sofronios. Ibid. Pg. 15-16

PART IV

1. *"You and him alone"*
(Mt. 18:15)

"*L*et everyone look at their hump and cover the mistakes of others with love" (Folk saying)

"*If your brother sins against you, go and tell him his fault between you and him alone*" (Mt. 18:15). The doctor doesn't look to find out how or why we got sick, but he looks at how to heal us and do us good. You must do the same; to heal your brother and not to take revenge. If you heal him, "*you have gained your brother*" (Mt. 18:15). And for your success, you will be forgiven many sins (Ja. 5:20).

"*But if he will not hear, take with you one or two more, that by the mouth of two or three witnesses every word may be established. And if he refuses to hear them, tell it to the church*" (Mt. 18:16-17),[34] to the "representatives" of the Church, to the Priests,[35] "*you shall come to the priests*" (Deut. 17:9).

"*Go and tell him his fault between you and him alone*" (Mt. 18:15), Jesus says. He doesn't want us to declare to everyone the sins of our brothers.

---

[34] When Jesus said these words He had in mind the following Mosaic Law: "*If a matter arises which is too hard for you to judge... then you shall arise and go up to the place which the Lord your God chooses. And you shall come to the priests..., that man shall die. So you shall put away the evil from Israel*" (Deut. 17:8-12).

[35] St. John Chrysostom. Homily 60 on the Gospel of Matthew. P.G. 58: 586

Why then, my dear, do you broadcast your brother's sins? Is it to honor your brother or to humiliate him? Think: *"We turn more to those who reveal the sins of the others than to those who committed the sins!"* [36]

By making their sins public, we provoke scandal to our brother's souls. And Jesus said: *"But whoever causes one of these little ones who believe in Me to sin, it would be better for him if a millstone were hung around his neck, and he were drowned in the depth of the sea"* (Mt. 18:6). *"Therefore, if he who scandalizes just one soul is worthy of death, what punishment does one deserve who scandalizes thousands of souls?"* [37]

The fathers of the desert say:
"Whenever we cover our brother's sin, God will also cover ours." [38]
"The sponge washes and cleans the dirt. We must be like the sponge: we must cover the mistakes of others. Whoever does it, cleanses and shines his soul, and rises up very high!" [39]

---

[36] St. John Chrysostom, Homily 31 on Acts. P.G. 60:234
[37] St. John Chrysostom. On the ambiguity of the Old Testament P.G. 56:190-1
[38] Gerontikon, Abbas Poemen, 64
[39] St. Joseph the Hesychast. Epistle 38.

A myth of Aesop:

"What evil do you think I do? I just prey on someone's chickens! That's all!" said the fox, criticizing himself.

"And what do you say I do? I prey on someone's lambs!" said the wolf, criticizing himself.

"And I, what do you say I do? When I carry grass for my boss, and I'm hungry, I secretly take a bite on some grass," said the donkey.

"Shame on you! You ate someone else's grass!" The fox and the wolf said to the donkey!

2. About judgment

St. John Chrysostom: *"I give you golden advice: if you want to judge, judge yourself, as the tax-collector did, and you will be saved."* [40]

Judgment is prohibited when we speak evil of our brethren when we condemn him. Because only one has the right to condemn, and that is Jesus Christ. *"There is one Lawgiver, who is able to save and to destroy. Who are you to judge another?"* (Ja. 4:12). *"To judge others is a shameless misuse of the Divine prerogative."* [41] *"Where do you order him to be put, into Paradise or into Hell?"* Said an angel of God to a Monk who condemned a brother. [42]

"Judge with righteous judgment" (Jn. 7:24). This kind of judgment is allowed when the law of the Lord is disregarded. Saint Basil the Great says:
"It is necessary to defend the Lord's commandments. Otherwise, we will also be convicted with those who violate them. The Corinthians knew that their brother was sinning, and they did not say anything. And St. Paul rebuked them: And you are puffed up, and have not rather mourned, that he who has done this deed might be taken away from among you" (1 Cor. 5:2).[43]

---

[40] On the ambiguity of the Old Testament. P.G. 56: 188
[41] St. John of the Ladder. Step. 10, on slander, 15
[42] Gerontikon. Abbas Isaac the Thevaios, 2
[43] St. Basil the Great. Terms on Epitome. Question 164. P.G. 31:1189-1192

They had to criticize him, to say that what he was doing was against the law of the Lord and that it was a sin.

There are two more cases on how one should deal with the errors, the sins of another.[44]

First case: When we have to discuss it so that we can correct our brother (Mt. 18:15-18). In this case, silence is considered a sin. *"Why did you keep silent? How did you get into it? Why did you not tell it to the Priest? You will be judged for your silence,"* St. Chrysostom states.[45]

Second Case: When we must protect our brother, who is associated with a dangerous man. St. Paul wrote to Timothy: *"Alexander the coppersmith did me much harm. May the Lord repay him according to his works. You also must beware of him, for he has greatly resisted our words"* (2 Tim. 4:14-15).

In these cases, we announce the sin of the other in an "apathetic"[46] manner, without feeling "sinful" joy within us, because this is not a case of the condemnation of another.

---

[44] St. Basil the Great. Terms on Epitome. Question 25. P.G. 31: 1.100

[45] St. John Chrysostom. To those who abandoned the church. P. G. 56: 270 & Canon 25 of the Council of Ancyra. & Canon 71 of St. Basil the Great.

[46] St. Maximus the Confessor. Evergetinos. Case 49. Chapter 6.

3. Why do we Judge?

A lady, while she was sitting on her balcony, looked down at the street and saw a young man walking. *"Wow...!,"* she said to me, *"how fat is this kid...!"* The young man was approaching her house. And it was her son...! She then told me: *"In no way is my son that fat."* Yet it was her son that was fat! *"The slander puts on the appearance of love and is the ambassador of an unholy and unclean heart."* [47]

"Do men gather grapes from thorn bushes or figs from thistles?" (Mt. 7:16). Thorn bushes and thistles represent passions in people. Like the thorn bushes produce thorny branches, and thistles produce prickly flowers, these people produce passions: judgment, slander, insult, etc. In other words, condemnation is a consequence (sickness) of our nature; that is why when seeing something provocative, we are instinctively driven to condemnation.

That is also why when we criticize someone, we feel a passionate, sinful pleasure. Our passions found their food!

Abbas Cassian once spoke to a group of Monks. He talked to them about living spiritually, about prayer, vigil, etc. The Monks began to fall asleep. Cassian wanting to show them that their sleep was demonic energy, he changed the subject and began speaking about earthly, vain things! Immediately the Monks woke up in a good mood![48]

---

[47] St. John of the Ladder. Step 10. On slander , 1
[48] Gerontikon. Abbas Cassian, 6

The devil made them fall asleep and then woke them up. He did what was good for him. Even this simple conversation about earthly things was pleasing to the devil. The passionate nature of the Monks did find its delicious food. Accordingly, it was enough for the devil that the Monks stopped hearing spiritual things! They killed their souls by hearing vain things!

What applies to us? What do we want to hear? Spiritual or secular things? Things concerning money, food, vocations, etc., or things concerning the salvation of our soul? What do we listen to more carefully, the accusations against our brother or the praises for our brother?

"How long, O you sons of men, Will you turn my glory to shame? How long will you love worthlessness and seek falsehood?" (Ps. 4:2).

4. The bitter fruits of judgment

" *T*he Pharisee was a keeper of divine law. He had good deeds: alms, fasts, prayers; that is why the people admired him. But because he condemned the tax-collector, who was already known to the world for his sins, he was punished by God, even though he told the truth! Therefore, when we condemn others who are not known to the world, what will be our reward? What would be our justification to God?" [49]

The most important:

"A sin may be small, but if he who does it criticizes another who does the same sin, then the small sin becomes big and unforgivable! God will punish him, not based on the nature of sin, but on the hard condemnation that he did to the other who fell into the same sin! He could receive twice and even three times as much punishment! This is what Jesus meant by saying: For with what judgment you judge, you will be judged; and with the measure you use, it will be measured back to you" (Mt. 7:2). [50]

Recall: when we criticize someone, we feel a passionate, sinful pleasure. Our passions found their food! And the more we judge, the more we feed our passions, and so on. "Slander is a leech lurking unfelt, wasting and draining the blood of charity. It is...the ruin of chastity." [51]

---

[49] St. John Chrysostom, Homily 2nd on Priscilla and Aquila P.G.51:204
[50] St. John Chrysostom, Homily 2nd on Priscilla and Aquila P.G.51:204
[51] St. John of the Ladder. Step 10. On slander , 1

St. John of the Ladder: *"Once I found myself outside the cell of a hermit. As I was sitting outside, I heard the Monks fighting with one another. They spoke bitterly and with anger against a Monk who was absent. Like partridges in a nest, they were railing against the other monk. One would have thought that the other monk was present. I advised them to abandon the hermit life and to go to a Monastery so that they don't end up becoming demons...!"* [52]

How to beat the judgment?

What helps us overcome the slander is to deal with our sins. In the hospital, every sick person looks only at his own illness, and he tries to get cured. So, should we! If we do, we will not bother with the sins of others. *"O Lord and King grant me to see my failings and not condemn my brother."* You see, the first, *"grant me to see my failings,"* brings the second *"and not condemn my brother."*

A Monk once said: *"I know that I was a lazy Monk, but I didn't judge anyone; thus, I will not be judged by the Lord. Therefore, I leave this world with joy!"* [53]

"Judge not, and you shall not be judged. Condemn not, and you shall not be condemned" (Lk. 6:37).

---

[52] St. John of the Ladder. Step 8. On freedom from anger and on meekness, 20
[53] Evergetinos, vol. III. Case 2. Chapter 8, 1

An Elder said:

On the great day of the judgment, there will be three surprises:

"Firstly, many who saw their sinful self and thought they were condemned will see themselves going to Paradise!

Secondly, many who actually were sure that they were going to Paradise, will see themselves going to Hell.

Thirdly, many who were certain of going to Hell, will see themselves going to Paradise!"

Let us, therefore, not become judges of the world.

5. Judging the Priests

"*Do not touch My anointed ones*" (Ps. 105:15), says the Lord. Meaning: Don't judge, don't condemn, don't harm My Priests! *"Do not accuse your priests, my brothers; an accusation against your priest is like to burn yourself."* [54]

What were the Scribes and the Pharisees? Perverted. Enemies of Christ. They were also successors of Moses. *"The Scribes and the Pharisees sit in Moses' seat,"* Jesus told the multitudes and His disciples (Mt. 23:1-2).

Due to the fact that they were Moses' successors, Christ required the world to respect them! [55] *"Therefore whatever they tell you to observe, that observe and do"* (Mt.23: 3). And the Priests are successors of Christ...!

King Saul became envious of David and searched and tried to kill him. David was given an opportunity for revenge, but he consciously chose not to harm King Saul and ordered his troops to do the same. In addition, David did not accuse King Saul of anything, in spite of the fact that King Saul was unjustly trying to kill him. *"For he is the Lord's anointed"* (1 Sam. 24:6), said David. And as a result of his stance, God honored him. [56] Despite lacking nobility, he became a Prophet and a king of Israel! [57]

---

[54] St. Kosmas the Etolos. Sermon B'2.
[55] St. John Chrysostom, Homily 2 on Priscilla and Aquila P.G. 51: 205
[56] St. John Chrysostom, Homily 2 on Priscilla and Aquila, P.G. 51:205
[57] St. John Chrysostom, Homily 2 on Priscilla and Aquila, P.G. 51:205

By "defending" your Priest (like David did concerning King Saul), you shield *"the Lord's anointed,"* and you may expect God's abundant blessings throughout your life.

St. John Chrysostom considers it "self-evident" for Christians to defend the Priesthood. He states: *"How can you stand in silence when someone offends a Priest? How can you not be angered? Why don't you shut them up? You will need to justify yourself on Judgment Day for this tolerance and silence!"* [58]

He (St. John Chrysostom) assigns this "duty" to the monks, as the flag-bearers. Otherwise, they will have then already failed in their spiritual mission.[59]

---

[58] St. John Chrysostom, Homily 2 on Priscilla and Aquila, P.G. 51:205
[59] St. John Chrysostom, To the blessed Philogonio, P.G. 48:752

6. Archangel Michael

" *Yet Michael the Archangel, in contending with the devil, when he disputed about the body of Moses, dared not bring against him a reviling accusation, but said, "The Lord rebuke you!"* (Jude, 9).

When Moses, the Leader of the Israelite's had died, the devil, wanting to deceive them, tried to grab his dead body, enter it and enliven it, to deceive the Israelites that he is Moses. But he was finally prevented from doing so by Archangel Michael. And a dispute broke out between them. Archangel Michael dared not bring against him a reviling accusation, but instead said, *"The Lord rebuke you!"* (Jude. 9) [60]

St. Nicodemus the Hagiorite interprets:

Archangel Michael respected the glory and the honor that God had given to the devil. Therefore He (Archangel) did not dare to bestow anything offensive on the devil, but simply said to him, *"The Lord rebuke you!"*. This implies as human beings, especially as Christians, we have no right to offend our worst enemy, even the devil.

And if we have not the right to offend the devil, accordingly, we have no right to offend the living "images of God," that is, our fellow brethren. Leave well enough alone the Christians, the Priests, and the High Priests!

---

[60] The devil can even "fabricate" resurrections of the dead...! Not that he can conquer death, because death was only conquered by Christ, but to deceive us he does something else: since he cannot "insert" himself in the soul of the deceased person, he himself enters the dead body and resurrects it...! He then imitates the movements and speech of the deceased person...! He tried to do this with Moses' dead body.

If (continues St. Nicodemus) Archangel Michael did not dare say anything against the devil, how much more can we say against heretics and idolaters! This is something that not even the Angels do before God. " *Whereas angels, who are greater in power and might, do not bring a reviling accusation against them before the Lord"* (2 Pet. 2:11).[61]

And by offending the heretics, the unbelievers, and the idolaters, we have the illusion that we have a mission!

---

[61] St. Nicodemus the Hagiorite. Explanation on the Seven Catholic Epistles. "Orthodox Kypsely" 1986. p. 691-696. Explanation on verse 9 of the Epistle of Juda

7. "As you want ..."

"*And just as you want men to do to you, you also do to them likewise*" (Lk. 6:31).

Consider, there is a friendly company, and you are absent. Then someone starts talking about you. What would you like him to say about you? Sure, you wouldn't like him to blame you. But even if he starts blaming you, you would expect the others to support you. Yes or no?

Just as you want the others to talk about you, you also talk about them likewise. *"See thou never do to another what thou wouldst hate to have done to thee by another."* [62]

Well? How do you talk about others? For example, what would you say about your colleague in his absence? Do you praise him? If someone starts criticizing him, how will you react? Will you stop it? Or will you follow him? Definitely, you will follow him!

There will be a common front against your colleague against a brother in Christ. And when you see him walking on the street, will you hurry to greet him, saying *"Hi my friend! How are you?"*

The hypocrisy will be even greater if you have accused your Priest! On one side, you revere him in public, you ask for his blessing, to pray for you, etc., and on the other side, you criticize and revile him amongst your friends, your family, and elsewhere? [63]

---

[62] Tobit 4:15
[63] St. John Chrysostom, Homily 2 on Priscilla and Aquila. P.G. 51:206

Pay attention: You want to accuse the others, and the others to praise you! Do you want to be praised by the others? Praise the others as well. But you want others to do for you, what you have not done for them...! You can blame them, but they cannot blame you! They must be mindful of you with extra-ordinary care!

St. Nectarios of Pentapolis: *"Love the others, so that the others may love you."*

PART V

1. *"False witness"*

" *You* shall not bear false witness against your neighbor" (Ex. 20:16)

In the Old Testament, the word "liar" means "deceiver," "unjust," etc. *"A poor man is better than a liar "* (Pr. 19:22). Thus, when the Lord commands, *"You shall not bear false witness against your neighbor"* (Ex. 20:16), He means don't say anything to deceive your neighbor, imitating the devil who deceived Adam and Eve (Gen. 3:5).

However, this does not mean that when a lie is not accompanied with the deception of your neighbor, that we have the right to lie to them. *"Therefore, putting away lying, let each one of you speak truth with his neighbor, for we are members of one another."* (Eph. 4:25). *"Does the eye fool the foot or the foot the eye? If the eye were to see a wild beast or a serpent on the road, will it lie to the foot that there is no serpent or beast at all? No! It will immediately inform the foot. So, we, as members of the same body, must do and say the truth one to another."* [64]

That is, when a member does not belong to our body, such as our brotherhood, our family, our parish, or our monastery, etc., we are not obligated to tell them the truth about ourselves, but we should not lie to them; we should just not answer them.

---

[64] St. John Chrysostom. Homily 14 on Ephesians P.G. 62: 100.

"We do not know" (Mt. 21:27), the Pharisees answered Jesus for something He asked them (Mt. 21:24-26). And yet they knew the answer! However, when the Pharisees asked Christ something (Mt. 21:23-24), Christ did not say to them, *"I do not know,"* instead, He said, *"neither will I tell you"* (Mt.21:27), teaching us to avoid lying.

As people with passions, we maneuver like the Pharisees. Lying is part of our nature, so it comes naturally and instinctively into our mouths. Yes!

No passionate person in this world tells the truth unless it benefits him. A child says to his father what benefits him, and a husband says to his wife what benefits him; even in confession, we say what benefits us.

However, there are some cases where a lie is preferable to the truth! We will see this next.

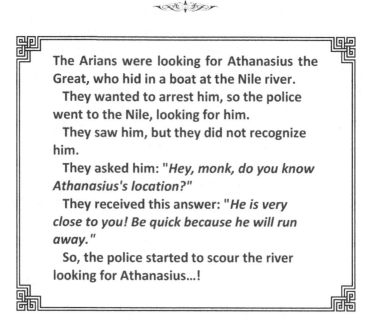

The Arians were looking for Athanasius the Great, who hid in a boat at the Nile river.

They wanted to arrest him, so the police went to the Nile, looking for him.

They saw him, but they did not recognize him.

They asked him: *"Hey, monk, do you know Athanasius's location?"*

They received this answer: *"He is very close to you! Be quick because he will run away."*

So, the police started to scour the river looking for Athanasius...!

2. A holy lie

St. John Chrysostom states that whoever uses a "lie" to benefit their neighbor; this does not count as a sin. *"Anyone who does such things should be praised and should not be condemned."* [65]

St. Basil the Great conveys the same message with the same essence, and he adds: It is a sin if someone is being unjust to their neighbor. An example from the Bible:

"The king of Egypt spoke to the Hebrew midwives..."When you do the duties of a midwife for the Hebrew women... if it is a son, then you shall kill him... But the midwives feared God, and did not do as the King of Egypt said ...So the King of Egypt called for the midwives and said to them, "Why have you done this thing...?" "Because the Hebrew women are not like the Egyptian women; for they are lively and give birth before the midwives come to them." (Ex. 1:15-19). They lied to the King! *"Therefore God dealt well with the midwives"* (Ex.1:20)."These *women midwives are worthy of praise,"* states St. Basil the Great.[66]

Another example from the life of the Fathers of the desert:

An Elder was living in the desert with a Monk. Soon, another Elder came to this desert who had a reputation of being a saint. The Elder, who was already in the desert, had a second cell and gave it to him to stay.

People learned that this holy Elder moved to the desert, and they started flocking to receive his blessing. The first Elder started to envy him. *"I have been here for so many years,"* he

---

[65] Logos 1st on Priesthood. P.G. 48: 629
[66] Homily 12 on the beginning of the Proverbs, 12. P.G. 31: 412

thought, *"and no one has come to see me! Look at how many people are coming to see him!"*

He ordered to his Monk:

-*"Tell the Elder to leave the soonest. I need the cell."*

-*"My Elder wants to know, how you are doing?"* The Monk said to him.

-*"I ask for his blessing. I'm a bit sick,"* he answered.

-*"What did he say? Will he leave?"* The Elder asked the Monk.

-*"He is looking for another cell...!"*

Two days passed, and the Elder was still in his cell. The owner took it more seriously. He said to his Monk:

-*"Go and tell him that if he doesn't leave the cell, I'll kick him out with my rod."*

-*"My Elder heard that you are sick and is sad. He sent me to see how you are doing!"* the Monk told the (holy) Elder. And he answered:

-*"Tell him that with his blessings, I have recovered."*

-*"What did he say? When will he leave?"* the Elder asked his Monk.

-*"God willing, he'll be leaving by Sunday...!"*

Sunday came, and the (holy) Elder was still in the cell. The owner grabbed his rod and was going to the cell to beat him (!) and kick him out (!) of his cell...! His Monk said to him:

-*"Let me go ahead of you to see if there are people in his cell, as otherwise, it will be embarrassing for us!"*

- *Go!*

-*"Because you got sick and you need care, my Elder is coming to take you to his cell...!"* said the Monk.

The (holy) Elder was so surprised that he came out of his cell to welcome him! While he was still far away, he made a prostration to him, shouting out loud: *"Oh my Elder! Don't get tired of me! I'm coming to see you...!"*

The owner was shocked...! He threw away his rod and ran to the holy Elder. He embraced him and took him to his cell!

Then he privately asked his disciple. *"You didn't tell him everything that I was telling you?"* *"No...!"* The elder fell to his feet. He said to his disciple: *"From now on, you will be my Elder and I, your disciple. Because of what you did, both of our souls were saved."* [67]

The Monk was *"wise as serpents and harmless as doves"* (Mt. 10:15).

---

[67] Evergetinos. Vol. 1. Case 37. Chapt. I,1.

3. Curses

The Lord wants us to pray for our enemy and not to curse him. *"Bless those who curse you and pray for those who spitefully use you"* (Lk. 6:28). But passions often cause a weaker man to violate the Lord's command, and instead of praying for his enemy, he curses him. And *"like a flitting sparrow, like a flying swallow, so a curse without cause shall not alight."* (Pr. 26:2). However, if we curse with cause, then things change.

"You shall not afflict any widow or fatherless child. If you afflict them in any way, and they cry at all to Me, I will surely hear their cry" (1Thes. 5:27). That is, whoever does wrong to a widow or a fatherless child, or even to anyone, and in their pain, they cry out to God, for example, to burn down that person's house, etc., God will hear them!

We have seen many examples where people have been afflicted, and they cursed, and their curse was cast just as they said! Parents have cursed their children, and their curse was cast just as their parents had said. Priests have cursed their flock, and their curse was cast just as they said.

Fr. Lambros S. (died in 1982) from the village Neohori (Arta), was driven to curse a woman. He mentioned to me:

"This woman wherever she went, she reproached me without any reason. She humiliated me in front of the whole village. The old men and women of the village advised her many times not to judge me, but she persisted.

One day, I found her outside the church. Even then, she continued to criticize me. I was angry, and, in my rage, I told her: "Now you will learn what it means to criticize a priest: I Hope your son croaks!"

As she was holding her child in her hand, immediately he fell and died! Then she became insane. She walked around the village like a crazy person until she died."

Since then, Fr. Lambros intensely prayed to God, asking for His forgiveness until the day he died.

If someone has cast a curse or has bound himself either by swearing an oath or with anathema, let him go the priest. And the priest will read for him the special prayers, and he will be loosened.

4. Oath and anathema

Are we allowed to take an oath in the Lord's name? There is no Holy Canon that forbids taking such an oath. There is simply one Canon that *"subjects to penalties those who take heathen oaths, and we decree to them ex-communication."* [68]

Saint Nektarios of Pentapolis teaches us that, according to the Bible, taking an oath in the Lord's name is considered a legal artifact.[69] Examples: In order for Saint Paul to become credible with the epistles he wrote, he called upon God as his witness, *"God is witness"* (1 Thes. 2:5). And *"I charge you by the Lord that this epistle be read to all the holy brethren"* (1 Thess. 2:27). Also, the Holy Fathers from the Fifth Ecumenical Council examined the Priests under oath on the Holy Gospel. [70]

St. Gregory Palamas says, however, that taking an oath should be avoided. Nevertheless, if someone is forced to take an oath, they should carry out many prayers, alms, and fasting so they can be forgiven by God, because they are transgressing His commandment that says you shall not take an oath under any circumstances.[71]

The eternally memorable theologian Nikolaos Sotiropoulos stated there are two types of oaths: an assertory oath and a promissory oath. With the first, you declare that you are saying the truth. This type of oath is allowed. With the second, you

---

[68] Quinisext Council. Canon 94
[69] Orthodox Holy Catechism. "Rigopoulos", pp. 112,126,127.
[70] Meletios Metropolitan of Niccpolis. The Fifth Ecumenical Council. Athens 1985 pg. 380,488
[71] Filokalia, v. 4. Decalog of the legislation according to Christ.

promise that you will abide by what you have sworn. For instance, if a Public Official has been elected, he is sworn into office on the Holy Bible that he will abide by the laws governing the city.

However, this type of oath should not be taking place since it's not certain that these promises will be kept. It would be best that the "Swearing-in Ceremony" would be replenished by something else that involves the fulfillment of their "wishes" towards their observance of the Laws.

To swear either on your life or on your children's life is a sin. Because you don't have authority either of yourself or others since we all belong to the Lord. Here is an example:

A lady went shopping at a grocery store. Thinking that she had paid, she prepared to leave. Then the shopkeeper said, *"You didn't pay me." "I paid you." "No, you didn't pay me." "Yes, I did pay you." "No, you didn't pay me." "For my life, I paid you!"* And immediately, the lady died. The money was found in her hand...!

Anathema

"And all the children of Israel complained against Moses and Aaron, and the whole congregation said to them, "If only we had died in the land of Egypt! Or if only we had died in this wilderness!" (Nu.14:2).

It was an anathema that they gave to themselves. And God listened to them! *"I the Lord have spoken this; I will surely do so to all this evil congregation who are gathered together against me...In this wilderness they shall be consumed, and there they shall die"* (Nu. 14:35).

Then they realized how great a sin it is to complain against God!

5. When you are blamed

"*As long we live, they offer us thorns, when we die roses*" (A. France)

He who blames you reveals the content of his heart. But you can also reveal the content of your heart if you blame him back. Then what makes you different from him? You are copying him!

You will say, *"I blamed him because he blamed me."* However, he who blamed you committed the sin, not you. You will not be judged by the words that others say about you, but by the words you say about others. Now then, when you return the offending action of blame-for-blame, then you have sinned! You will also be judged!

"Love your enemies, do well to those who hate you, bless those who curse you, and pray for those who spitefully use you" (Lk. 6:27-28). Well, does this divine commandment apply to you too? If so, why do you not keep it?

If praise *"increases the gall of passions,"*[72] then the accusations cleanse the soul from the gall of passions. It is the best detergent! Therefore, if you struggle, the blame that you accepted, it actually will clean your soul (while on the other side, the one who blamed you, he darkened his soul!).

St. John of the Ladder said: *"You should believe the popular saying that reproof is the washtub for the passions of the soul. For*

---

[72] St. John of the Ladder. Step 4, on obedience, 103

when people in the world overwhelm someone to his face with in-dignities and then boast of this before others, they say: "I gave him a washing." And this is perfectly true." [73]

St. John Chrysostom: *"If you will be blamed by your enemy for something bad that you have done to him, and you will be silent, you will sigh, and ask God to forgive your sin. You will immediately be forgiven. For example, because the tax-collector did not react to the accusations he heard from the Pharisees, but was silent, God had forgiven his sins. So, you see how much you gain when you confront the blames with patience and bravery?"* [74]

"You benefit much more when your enemies blame you, than you do when your friends praise you." [75]

This does not mean that every one of us should accept any kind of blame that may come our way. Take, for example, if someone is a missionary, he must defend himself so that those who follow him will not be scandalized. At the same time, he must pray for his accusers to be forgiven by God.

---

[73] St. John of the Ladder. Step 8, on freedom from anger, 28
[74] St. John Chrysostom. Homily 3 on David and Saul. P.G.54: 700-1
[75] St. John Chrysostom. Homily 3 on David and Saul, P.G. 54: 700

An Abbot of a Monastery cried out wildly to a humble Monk. Then the Monk ran to the kitchen, prepared some tea, and brought it to the Abbot.

- *Who told you that I needed tea?!* The Abbot asked him.

- *As you were shouting at me, I noticed that your voice was becoming hoarse...!*

"Brethren, do not be children in understanding; however, in malice be babes, but in understanding be mature" (1 Cor. 14:20).

6. Mouth and Holy Communion

" *W*ith it we bless our God and Father, and with it we curse men, who have been made in the similitude of God. Out of the same mouth proceed blessing and cursing" (Ja. 3:9-10).

And with this same mouth, we receive the Holy Communion. *"My brethren, these things ought not to be so"* (Ja. 3:10).

Saint Basil says that daily Holy Communion is *"good and beneficial."* [76] But that applies only to the pure ones. Namely, if your mouth is not pure, you can't receive daily Holy Communion. It is not good and beneficial!

He (St Basil the Great) says: Anyone who censured another should be suspended from taking Holy Communion for one week; the same also applied to anyone that tolerated to listen to a person censuring another; *"both are excommunicated."* [77]

Which person living in this world is clear of such sins?

St. John Chrysostom considers anyone that criticizes a Priest as being unworthy of passing through the Temple's outer door. [78] Even more so when it comes to communing Christ's Body and Blood. Moreover:

If a person that calls his brother a "fool" is condemned to *"hell fire"* (Mt. 5:22), therefore is unworthy to receive Holy Communion; just imagine how reprehensible is a person that inundates another with terrible insults! *"A person insulting another is even*

---

[76] Letter to the Patrician of Caesarea P.G. 32: 484
[77] Terms in an Epitome. Question 26. P.G. 31:1101& About Penances, P.G. 31:1305-1316
[78] Homily 2 on Priscilla and Aquila, P.G. 51: 204

more unclean than a dog that rolls in its own vomit!" [79] says St. John Chrysostom. He went so far as to say that he would prefer to administer Holy Communion to a person that consumes excrement rather than a person with a vile mouth...! [80]

And if someone with a "dirty" mouth receives Holy Communion, what will happen to him? What happened to the Corinthians? (1 Cor. 11:27-29). They did not examine themselves, and they hurriedly partook of Holy Communion: *"for this reason many are weak and sick among you, and many sleep"* (1 Cor. 11:30).

Without self-examination, Holy Communion is fearful and dreadful...!

---

[79] Homily 2 on Acts of the Apostles 31, P.G. 60: 233
[80] Homily on Acts of the Apostles 31. P.G. 60: 233

EPILOGUE

1. Bloodless Martyrs

Saint Ephraim, the Hagiorite, lived an ascetic life in the remote area of Katounakia on Mt. Athos for over fifty years. He has said the following from his ascetical experience:

"The first and foremost enemy of man is not the devil but man himself; his passions. Therefore, his big struggle is to defeat himself.

Martyrs, therefore, are not only those whose heads have been cut off because they refused to deny Jesus, but there are other types; they are bloodless martyrs.

They are unknown to the world but known only to the Lord. The martyrs bloodied for their faith were martyred once, while the other type martyrs every day."

Every day they cut off something which brings pleasure to their passionate nature. They crush the gratification, which comes from the satisfaction of sensual pleasures. Can we even imagine something like this? Remember:

When we judge someone, we feel a certain kind of pleasure. (If we felt sorrow, we would not judge!). So, if we stop judging, it is like to stop feeling this pleasure! It is an unpleasant and undesirable condition for our passionate nature! But as Christians, we must do the undesirable. *"Narrow is the gate and difficult is the way which leads to life, and there are few who find it"* (Mt. 7:14).

Things are even worse when we are being criticized or blamed. Instead of feeling pleasure, we feel pain. This pain makes us want to explode, so we can lessen the pain and satisfy our passions. In so doing, we violate the command of the Lord that tells us, *"bless those who curse you, pray for those who abuse you"* (Lk. 6:28).

Thus, as Christians, we must close our mouth and not say anything against our brother, who judges and insults us. As a result, we increase the pain in our hearts.

Abbas Achilles was blamed, held his tongue, his spiritual wound grew, and he endured suffering. The result? He literally spat blood![81] You can only imagine his psychological pain and his struggle to tame this "beast," the tongue!

King David was hovering before the face of his enemies. He said: *"I was mute with silence ... And my sorrow was stirred up!"* (Ps. 39:2). *"For Your sake we are killed all day long; we are accounted as sheep for the slaughter"* (Ps. 44:22). That is, every day, he harmonized his life according to the words of the Lord. Every day he would renounce his will to serve the Lord!

The same circumstances applied to St. Paul. He said: *"For Your sake we are killed all day long; we are accounted as sheep for the slaughter"* (Rom. 8:36).

Do we dare kneel in front of the Crucified Jesus and say to Him, *"For your sake we are killed all day long?"* Do we?

---

[81] Gerontikon. Abbas Achilles, 4

2. *"What a shame!"*

"***W**hat a shame! To see an old man, going to a children's school is a great disgrace!"* [82]
And that old man can be ourselves...!

Have we ever thought about how many times we have gone to Church? How many times have we read the Scriptures or have heard sermons? How many times have we received Holy Communion?

After so many years of lessons in the church, we should have already become perfect, saints, tasting the fruits of the Holy Spirit: *"love, joy, peace, longsuffering, kindness, goodness, faithfulness, gentleness, self-control"* (Gal. 5:22-23).

But we always stay at the same spot; we have not climbed the first step towards a so-called spiritual life. We are permanently below the first step. We are like strangers in our own home, in our Church. We are in danger of making a Church without Christ! And consequently, we do not keep the Lord's commandments, which lead to perfection and sanctification.

Once again: *"Bless those who curse you and pray for those who spitefully use you"* (Lk. 6:28). Do we apply the Lord's commandment everywhere and always in our lives? If we had applied it, we would have gotten wings, and we would have soared high!

St. Silouanos, the Hagiorite says from his experience: *"It's a great thing to pray for those who offend you. The Lord will sanctify you, and by the Holy Spirit He will make you know Him (that is, the Lord). Then, and for His sake, you will endure with joy any*

---

[82] Step 26 On discernment of thoughts, passions and virtues

kind of sorrow. And not only this. The Lord will give you love for the whole world. You will wish good to all people, and you will pray for everybody as if you were praying for yourself!" [83]

And the problem with us is that instead of praying for our enemy, we offend and insult him! What would a non-Christian do differently?

You may say: *"If I lived on the Holy Mountain or in the Holy Land, I would become a saint."* That's not so.

It is not where you live, but how you go about struggling to keep the Lord's commandments, and this can be done anywhere!

"I want to go into the desert to be alone like a stranger," said Abbas Longinus to Abbas Loukio. *"If you don't watch your tongue, wherever you go, you will never be a stranger. If you control your tongue while living in the world, then you will be a stranger to the world."* [84]

"The heart of fools is in their mouth: but the mouth of the wise is in their heart." [85]

---

[83] The writings of St. Silouanos the Hagiorite. D, about peace. Ibid.
[84] Evergetinos. Vol. 3. Case 31, Chapter I,6
[85] The Wisdom of Jesus the son of Sirach 21:26

OTHER BOOKS BY
"ARCHANGELS PUBLICATIONS"

1. Tearful Eyes
2. Christian or an Actor?
3. The World's Final Call
4. A Monk's Adventure
5. Confronting the Devil
6. After Death
7. Great Christian Feasts
8. Forty Stormy Years
9. Battles & Passions. Anger, Hatred, Envy
10. Highly Favored One. The Life of Mariam

Author
Archimandrite Vassilios Bakoyiannis

Made in the USA
Monee, IL
15 April 2021